Read & Respond

FOR
KS2

CW00347472

Read & Respond

FOR
KS2

Author: Rob Walton

Development Editor: Simret Brar

Editor: Dodi Beardshaw

Assistant Editor: Sally Gray

Series Designer: Anna Oliwa

Designer: Rebecca Male

Text © Rob Walton © 2008 Scholastic Ltd

Designed using Adobe InDesign

Published by Scholastic Ltd,
Book End, Range Road, Witney,
Oxfordshire OX29 0YD

www.scholastic.co.uk

Printed by Bell & Bain

8 9   5 6 7

British Library Cataloguing-in-Publication Data
A catalogue record for this book is available from the British
Library.

ISBN 978-1407-10044-9

The rights of the author of this work have been asserted by him in
accordance with the Copyright, Designs and Patents Act 1988.

Extracts from the Primary National Strategy's *Primary
Framework for Literacy* (2006) www.standards.dfes.gov.uk/
primaryframework © Crown copyright. Reproduced under the
terms of the Click Use Licence.

All rights reserved. This book is sold subject to the condition
that it shall not, by way of trade or otherwise, be lent, hired out or
otherwise circulated without the publisher's prior consent in any
form of binding or cover other than that in which it is published
and without a similar condition, including this condition, being
imposed upon the subsequent purchaser.

No part of this publication may be reproduced, stored in a
retrieval system, or transmitted, in any form or by any means,
electronic, mechanical, photocopying, recording or otherwise,
without the prior permission of the publisher. This book remains
copyright, although permission is granted to copy pages where
indicated for classroom distribution and use only in the school
which has purchased the book, or by the teacher who has
purchased the book, and in accordance with the CLA licensing
agreement. Photocopying permission is given only for purchasers
and not for borrowers of books from any lending service.

Acknowledgements
The publishers gratefully acknowledge permission to reproduce
the follwing copyright material: **The Penguin Group Ltd** for the
use of text extracts from *The Diary of a Young Girl*: *Anne Frank*:
The definitive edition edited by Otto H. Frank and Mirjam
Pressler, translated by Susan Massoty © 1991, The Anne Frank-
Fonds, Basle, Switzerland (1997, Viking). English translation
© 1995, Doubleday, a division of Bantam Doubleday Dell
Publishing Group Inc. (1995, Viking).

The Diary of a Young Girl

About the book

The Diary of a Young Girl, popularly referred to as *The Diary of Anne Frank*, was started when Anne was a 13-year-old girl in hiding from the Nazis. She was to continue to write to Kitty, her imaginary friend, for the next two years.

The scattered pages of the Diary were saved by Miep Gies, one of the family's helpers, and Anne's father arranged for it to be published in 1947. Fifty years later the so-called definitive version was published, restoring much material that had been omitted from the earlier version.

Since publication it has been one of the world's most widely read books. It is a popular book for many reasons. Part of its enduring appeal is because people can identify with the everyday concerns of this teenager, who details her day-to-day life against the background of hatred and prejudice brought by Nazism. Anne's hopes and aspirations are shared by many readers, and people empathise with her feelings for Peter, her ambitions to be a writer and the problems she faces with humour, spirit and resilience. There are also bleak and chilling moments in the book which both grip and move the reader.

There are countless images and details in Anne's Diary which resonate and stay with the reader long after the book has been read.

The treatment of the Jews, and of children in particular, makes for uncomfortable but essential reading. Some of the horrors described in the book have resurfaed to different extents and in different forms in many parts of the world.

About the author

Anne Frank was a Jewish girl born on June 12th, 1929 in Germany. During the Holocaust her family was forced to flee to Amsterdam in the Netherlands by the Nazis. On her thirteenth birthday she began to write her Diary. The following month she was forced into hiding. Anne, her sister Margot, parents Otto and Edith, along with four others, spent twenty-five months in hidden rooms above her father's office. In the 'Secret Annexe', Anne continued to write her Diary. Anne's writing was developing all the time she kept her Diary and she had ambitions

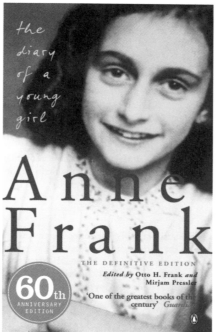

to be a writer. She had a talent for writing expressively and with humour and honesty. Her ability to laugh at herself, her situation and those around her is a particularly endearing quality. The difficulties she had with her family and the other people in the Annexe, especially her mother, were never resolved.

They were betrayed to the Nazis and in 1944 the Franks were sent to the Auschwitz concentration camp in Poland, where her mother died the following year. The sisters were moved to Bergen-Belsen in Germany in October 1944. In March 1945, Anne, aged 15, and Margot, aged 19, died of typhus at Bergen-Belsen.

Her father, Otto, was the only one of the eight people who hid in the 'Secret Annexe' to survive the war. Although Anne Frank died before her sixteenth birthday, her father fulfilled his daughter's wish to be a writer and her name is now known all over the world.

Facts and figures
The Diary of a Young Girl was first published in 1947. Since then it has been read by tens of millions of people all over the world.
It has been translated into 67 languages.
More than 31 million copies have been sold.
The Definitive Edition was published in 1995 in America.

Guided reading

Sunday, 14 June 1942

Before reading, ask the children what they expect from the book. Are they expecting it to be sad, enlightening, interesting, depressing, moving? Note these comments for future reference. Also ask if they have heard of the book previously and if they know anybody who has read it. Suggest they ask friends and family if they know anything about the book.

Ask the children to read to the end of the entry (explain this term), then ask them for their first impressions of Anne. Can they identify with her?

Have they noticed the use of brackets/ parentheses? (There are six examples, including two in one sentence.) When and why does Anne use this device? (She gives more information and talks even more directly to the reader: they come across as personal asides.)

Ask how Anne refers to the Diary ('you')and why? (This gives a personal, intimate effect.)

After reading this first section, do they think the text will appeal to both children and adults?

Sunday, 5 July & Wednesday, 8 July 1942

Ask the children to read the first of these entries. How do the opening paragraphs relate to their own experiences? Does this suggest the content of other parts of the Diary is relevant to children and adults today? (Even though Anne Frank was writing over sixty years ago, many of her concerns are the same as those of today's young people.)

Discuss the lines: 'Don't you worry. We'll take care of everything. Just enjoy your carefree life while you can.' Was Anne's dad being truthful or reassuring? Was he trying to make himself feel better or did he genuinely believe this? (There were limits to what the family could do to prevent the Nazi threat.)

Now ask the children to read the 8th July entry. Why has Anne written days after the event? (So much has been happening, and she packed her

Diary ready for the move.) Ask the children to note the passage of time and how and why Anne records it ('three o'clock...', 'around five o'clock...', 'until ten o'clock...', 'at seven-thirty'). There are several examples which help the reader to engage with both the urgency and the contradictory waiting around.

Wednesday, 7 October & Friday, 9 October 1942

Tell the children they are about to read two contrasting entries. As they read they should note the differences in tone and mood. What effect is created by having these two entries next to each other? (The first is light and amusing and serves to highlight the stark and depressing tone of the second. Anne's imaginary world is thrown into stark contrast with the truth of life outside the Annexe.)

Ask the children why they think Anne makes such an exhaustive list. (Is it to immerse herself even further in the fantasy as a way of escaping the harsh reality?)

Ask the children to find examples of negative language used in the second entry, and discuss its effect ('I feel terrible', 'heartrending', 'distraught', 'crippled', 'didn't dare'). It helps us to empathise with the family's plight.

Friday, 2 April & Tuesday, 27 April 1943

Read the entry and ask the children to consider how the tension between Anne and her mother develops during the extract. Note how the language changes. ('Mother... asked very gently', 'slowly walked', 'contorted with pain', 'tears slid down her cheeks' and so on.) How is Anne feeling? How can you tell? (Sorry for herself. Note the opening line and the reading of her father's unspoken words. How does this entry make the children feel about Anne? Do they sympathise or empathise (explain these terms)?

Ask the children to read the next entry. Why do they think there are sometimes gaps between the entries?

Challenge the children to find examples of figurative language ('the house is still trembling', 'I've got ants in my pants again', 'Register Office took an extra beating', 'I have bags under my eyes'). Which examples do the children think are most successful and why?

Wednesday, 3 November & Monday evening, 8 November 1943

Ask the children to read the first entry and note any tensions between the people in the Annexe. (There are clear tensions between Anne's family about Judaism and other matters, and there is also tension between the others – 'Dussel and the van Daans are still at loggerheads'.)

Ask the children if they always trust the quotations in the text. Do they think Anne would be able to remember exactly what people said and later write it in her Diary? Would the children be able to remember in this way? Would Anne's circumstances make it easier or harder to remember the things that happened and what was said in the Annexe? (Perhaps the close-knit group and the confinement itself make the experiences more acute and the detail easier to recall.)

Now ask the children to read the second entry. How does it build on the fears expressed in the previous entry? (Anne's imagination is focused on negative thoughts.)

Ask the children to read the last paragraph, noting the ways Anne talks of darkness, and discuss the impression this creates ('menacing black clouds', 'surrounded by darkness', 'dark mass of clouds'). These words, and these entries, have a more hopeless feel than many others. Anne sees little cause for optimism.

Sunday, 27 February & Monday, 28 February 1944

Tell the children that the first paragraph concerns Anne's feelings for Peter. Can they predict what might happen between them? Ask the children to discuss the significance of Anne writing 'everyone wishes I were miles away'. They are destined to stay in very close proximity, perhaps Anne wishes in some ways that she was miles away. She may dream of a future with Peter where they are a long way away from the Annexe.

Ask the children to read both extracts and note the adjectives Anne uses to describe herself. (In the first: 'unsure', 'vulnerable', 'noisy'. In the second: 'unhappy', 'sentimental', 'despondent', 'foolish'.) Which of these do they think best describes Anne and why?

Encourage the children to discuss why Anne writes she 'dreams' about Peter in the first entry, and says 'It's like a nightmare' in the second.

Have they noticed a difference in Anne's form of address in these entries? (She is now signing off as 'Anne M. Frank'.)

Wednesday, 29 March & Friday, 31 March 1944

Suggest that the children read the comments about Anne's Diary, and ask them to discuss their thoughts about the Diary as a whole. Anne writes 'ten years after the war people would find it very amusing to read how we lived...'. Ask the children what they think Anne means by 'amusing' and discuss why she wrote it. (Talk about the notion of hindsight and the value of contemporary documents.)

Ask the children to note and comment on the simile used in the second paragraph ('the houses trembled like blades of grass in the wind'). It is quite poetic, but probably not entirely successful.

Anne writes 'you still know very little about us'. To what extent do the children think this is true? Which characters do the children think

Guided reading

they know best and why is this? (Anne has given an insight on some level about all the residents.) Ask the children to read the second entry. How would they describe the mood or tone of this entry? (There are many notes of optimism, but she also talks about the Hungarian Jews being 'doomed'.)

Anne often uses lists in her writing. Have the children noticed any in these entries? (She lists stolen goods and catalogues reasons for low morale in the first entry. In the second she lists the presents for Mr van Daan's birthday.)

Tuesday, 1 August 1944

Explain that this is the final entry in Anne's Diary. Ask the children to read the whole entry and discuss how Anne is feeling about herself at this time. (She is being quite negative and feels misunderstood by those around her.)

Do the children think they have more of an understanding of her from the Diary? Is it possible for the children to have a better understanding of her feelings than those who have shared her living space for two years? (She confides in the Diary and thus the readers.)

Challenge the children to find several of the character traits which Anne attributes to herself. (There are several, from 'A bundle of contradictions' to 'happy-go-lucky' and 'pure'.) Anne discusses the two sides of her character at length. Which of the two do the children think comes across most clearly in this entry and in the Diary as a whole? What is the effect of this self-analysis as the last entry? Does it seem strange or fitting that the final entry is devoted to the writer talking about herself, and not the other characters or the situation in the Annexe or the outside world? Encourage the children to sum up their feelings about Anne and the Diary as succinctly as possible.

Shared reading

Extract 1

● Display an enlarged copy of Extract 1 so that all children can see it.
● Read the extract to the class and invite comments about the notion of the 'stiff upper lip' and smiling in the face of adversity. (This is what Anne talks about in the extract.)
● Ask the children to list the negative words used ('gruesome', 'dreadful', 'gloomy', 'melancholy', etc.) and write the positive words opposite them ('cheerful', 'joking', 'laughing').

● Invite suggestions about how Anne feels towards her family at this point. (She has already distanced herself from her mother and sister and is now losing faith in her father to offer her the support she needs.)
● Ask the children to find points in the extract when Anne asks herself/Kitty questions. ('And what would be the point of turning the Secret Annexe into a Melancholy Annexe? But am I supposed to spend the whole day crying?')

Extract 2

● Display an enlarged copy of Extract 2 so it is visible to all children.
● Read the extract to the class and ask if they believe that Anne is an 'honest-to-goodness teenager' – the last words in the extract. Ask them to justify their opinions.
● Anne says she will not describe quarrels in detail but goes on to write about a specific example. Choose a child to underline it. (Dussel using too much gravy.)
● Ask the children if they consider Anne's

feelings towards Dussel are reasonable. (They seem extreme, but confinement will lead to extremes. Her feelings are going to be amplified because of the extraordinary circumstances.)
● Challenge the children to highlight any phrases which suggest how Anne feels about the future. ('The war is going to go on...' and, 'I also believe that if I live here much longer...') Ask the children what this tells us about Anne's state of mind. (She seems quite negative.)

Extract 3

● Display an enlarged copy of Extract 3 so all children can clearly follow it.
● Read the Diary entry to the class and ask the children to identify interesting verbs in the opening sentences ('dashed', 'shoved', 'was squatting'). Circle the children's suggestions, and note how the drama is then heightened. (With 'shouts' and 'squeals'.)
● Ask the children to note how Anne conjures up a vivid image of the leak and its aftermath.

(By using the detail of the yellow drops falling between a pile of stockings and some books. Also by describing Peter being 'armed' with various cleaning materials. The reader has a clear picture.)
● Challenge the children to suggest why Anne wrote this particular entry. (Was she conscious of the need for light relief? Was she being a creative writer as well as a diarist?)

Extract 1

From FRIDAY, 20 NOVEMBER 1942

Dearest Kitty,

We don't really know how to react. Up till now very little news about the Jews had reached us here, and we thought it best to stay as cheerful as possible. Every now and then Miep used to mention what had happened to a friend, and Mother or Mrs van Daan would start to cry, so she decided it was better not to say any more. But we bombarded Mr Dussel with questions, and the stories he had to tell were so gruesome and dreadful that we can't get them out of our heads. Once we've had time to digest the news, we'll probably go back to our usual joking and teasing. It won't do us or those outside any good if we continue to be as gloomy as we are now. And what would be the point of turning the Secret Annexe into a Melancholy Annexe?

No matter what I'm doing, I can't help thinking about those who are gone. I catch myself laughing and remember that it's a disgrace to be so cheerful. But am I supposed to spend the whole day crying? No, I can't do that. This gloom will pass.

Added to this misery there's another, but of a more personal nature, and it pales in comparison to the suffering I've just told you about. Still, I can't help telling you that lately I've begun to feel deserted. I'm surrounded by too great a void. I never used to give it much thought, since my mind was filled with my friends and having a good time. Now I think either about unhappy things or about myself. It's taken a while, but I've finally realized that Father, no matter how kind he may be, can't take the place of my former world. When it comes to my feelings, Mother and Margot ceased to count long ago.

Extract 2

From SATURDAY, 15 JANUARY 1944

Mother's birthday is rapidly approaching. She received some extra sugar from Mr Kugler, which sparked off jealousy on the part of the van Daans, because Mrs van D. didn't receive any on her birthday. But what's the point of boring you with harsh words, spiteful conversations and tears when you know they bore us even more?

Mother has expressed a wish, which isn't likely to come true any time soon: not to have to see Mr van Daan's face for two whole weeks. I wonder if everyone who shares a house sooner or later ends up at odds with their fellow residents. Or have we just had a stroke of bad luck? At mealtimes, when Dussel helps himself to a quarter of the half-filled gravy boat and leaves the rest of us to do without, I lose my appetite and feel like jumping to my feet, knocking him off his chair and throwing him out of the door.

Are most people so stingy and selfish? I've gained some insight into human nature since I came here, which is good, but I've had enough for the present. Peter says the same.

The war is going to go on despite our quarrels and our longing for freedom and fresh air, so we should try to make the best of our stay here.

I'm preaching, but I also believe that if I live here much longer, I'll turn into a dried-up old beanstalk. And all I really want is to be an honest-to-goodness teenager!

Yours, Anne

Extract 3

From WEDNESDAY, 10 MAY 1944

Dearest Kitty,

We were sitting in the attic yesterday afternoon working on our French when suddenly I heard the splatter of water behind me. I asked Peter what it might be. Without pausing to reply, he dashed up to the loft – the scene of the disaster – and shoved Mouschi, who was squatting beside her soggy litter box, back to the right place. This was followed by shouts and squeals, and then Mouschi, who by that time had finished peeing, took off downstairs. In search of something similar to her box, Mouschi had found herself a pile of wood shavings, right over a crack in the floor. The puddle immediately trickled down to the attic and, as luck would have it, landed in and next to the potato barrel. The ceiling was dripping, and since the attic floor has also got its share of cracks, little yellow drops were leaking through the ceiling and on to the dining-table, between a pile of stockings and books.

I was doubled up with laughter, it was such a funny sight. There was Mouschi crouched under a chair, Peter armed with water, powdered bleach and a cloth, and Mr van Daan trying to calm everyone down. The room was soon set to rights, but it's a well-known fact that cat puddles stink to high heaven. The potatoes proved that all too well, as did the wood shavings, which Father collected in a bucket and brought downstairs to burn.

Poor Mouschi! How were you to know it's impossible to get peat for your box?

Plot, character and setting

Quick write

Objective: Appraise a text quickly, deciding on its value, quality or usefulness.
What you need: Copies of the Diary or copies of various entries, large sheets of paper.

What to do
● Tell the children they are going to look at certain Diary entries to find out about plot, character and setting. (Tuesday, 11th April 1944 is good for all three features. Choose other entries of an appropriate length.)
● Ask the children to discuss the techniques of skimming and scanning to find information.
● Now tell them they are going to be working in groups of three. One child will make notes about setting, one about plot and one about character.
● Explain that they will write on large sheets of paper.
● Challenge the children to write as quickly as possible.
● Hand out or point the children to a new Diary entry after five minutes.
● Repeat this formula three or four times.
● Bring the children together to find out which group has made the most sensible and useful notes.
● Ask the children how they tackled the task – did they underline or highlight, or write straight on to their sheet. Stress the importance of using a method which finds the information and works best for them as individuals.

Differentiation
For older/more confident learners: Offer individuals the opportunity to work on their own. They will be making notes on all three aspects.
For younger/less confident learners: Work with these children, supporting the reading and acting as scribe if necessary.

Plotting

Objective: Consider how a writer from a different time and place presents experiences.
What you need: Photocopiable page 15, copies of the Diary.

What to do
● Discuss the fact that *The Diary of a Young Girl* does not have a plot in the same way as other forms of writing, such as a story. In many ways Anne wrote down random thoughts, feelings and comments on the events in her life and the lives of those around her.
● Tell the children they are going to locate entries in the Diary which describe external events – those pertaining to the war in general and the treatment of Jews in particular. It is these events that provide much of the plot of the book.
● Talk about chronology: how the war develops, how Anne's relationships with Peter and the others develop.
● Show the children Photocopiable page 15, and instruct them to complete the boxes as described.
● Direct the children to certain entries: June 20th and November 19th, 1942; June 6th, July 15th and 21st, 1944. Note how Anne stays optimistic and hopeful at such times.
● Discuss how Anne presents her experiences and the different techniques she uses.

Differentiation
For older/more confident learners: Challenge the children to comment on the links between what happens outside and inside the Annexe. Are there any conclusions to be drawn about the way people tackle things domestically when things are going well or otherwise?
For younger/less confident learners: Provide a list of Diary entries including those outlined above.

Plot, character and setting

Speaking out

Objective: Make notes on and use evidence from across a text to explain events or ideas.
What you need: Copy of the Niemöller quotation, flipchart, copies of the Diary.

What to do
● Read aloud the following quotation attributed to Martin Niemöller. 'First they came for the communists and I did not speak out because I was not a communist. Then they came for the trade unionists and I did not speak out because I was not a trade unionist. Then they came for the Jews and I did not speak out because I was not a Jew. Then they came for me and there was nobody left to speak out for me.'
● Ask the children to discuss this in the context of Anne's Diary. Talk about the Holocaust and the Final Solution and their impact on the lives of children and adults in Germany and other countries.

● Discuss what happens to people in such situations: some are persecuted; some 'turn a blind eye'; others offer resistance.
● Ask the children to consider the people outside the Annexe who kept the secret and offered help. Record their suggestions on the flipchart.
● Now tell the children to use the text to make their own notes on incidents where help was given. Note the events such as moving into the Annexe, visitors and gifts.
● Together, discuss why this help was offered.

Differentiation
For older/more confident learners: Make notes on how the help changes through the two years of captivity. Are people constant or do the pressures of Nazism make it increasingly difficult to help?
For younger/less confident learners: Draw an outline of Bep, Miep or another character and inside the outline, write about the things they do.

Family matters

Objective: Interrogate texts to deepen and clarify understanding and response.
What you need: Photocopiable page 16, copies of the Diary, different writing implements.

What to do
● Tell the children they are going to be thinking about Anne's family. Now show them the Photocopiable page 16 and ask them to talk to their partner for two minutes about the 'Appearance' of Otto, Edith and Margot. Share this with the class, then do the same with 'Actions' and 'Talk'. Clearly explain that 'Appearance' can refer to their physicality, what they wear and how they move.
● Ask the children to write very brief notes in the boxes about the three characters. Allow ten minutes for this.
● Now bring the children back together, hand out copies of the Diary and different pens, and

tell them they are going to have another ten minutes to write. This time they should refer directly to the text for descriptions. They will be moving from general impressions to interrogating the text. You may direct them to certain entries, such as pages 41 and 50 as good starting points. Now ask them to complete the summaries.
● Together, discuss any changes the children made when they were able to refer to the text. Ask them to note if and how Anne's descriptions of her family change during the Diary.
● Read aloud some summaries to see if the children have drawn the same conclusions.

Differentiation
For older/more confident learners: Challenge the children to find passages which show aspects of 'Appearance', 'Actions' and 'Talk'.
For younger/less confident learners: Point the children to specific entries, such as page 41 for 'Talk'.

Plot, character and setting

Prospectus

> **Objective:** Explore how writers use language for comic and dramatic effects.
> **What you need:** Copies of Diary entry Tuesday, 17 November 1942.

What to do

● Show the children the Prospectus and Guide to the Secret Annexe from the above Diary entry.
● Ask the children to discuss the humour in this list of rules for those hiding in the Annexe. Why is it so funny and how could this humour be described?
● Discuss how this prospectus tells us lots about both the physical setting of the Annexe (the rooms and so on) and the setting in the historical context of Nazi persecution of the Jews.
● Discuss the formal language and conventions used, and how sticking to this makes the writing successful.

● Ask the children which parts of the prospectus they think are the most amusing, and ask them to explain their views.
● Ask the children how Germany and Germans are regarded in the prospectus.
● The rules and regulations are referred to as 'a van Daan production'. Who do the children think might have written them?
● Ask the children if they can think of other examples in the Diary when Anne and the others laugh in the face of adversity.

> **Differentiation**
> **For older/more confident learners:** Write a Prospectus and Guide to the Frank Family (or the van Daans) in the same style.
> **For younger/less confident learners:** Give the children copies of the text and ask them to highlight those parts which they find most amusing. Annotate the text with explanations about each point.

Word wall

> **Objective:** Explain how writers use expressive language to create images and atmosphere.
> **What you need:** Photocopiable page 17, enlarged copy of text, copies of text for children.

What to do

● Ask the children to look at the extract from Anne's Diary entry of 28 September 1942.
● Explain how atmosphere can contribute to the setting of a piece of writing. In this instance it adds flavour, as well as giving us insights into the character of Anne and those around her. By talking about the injustices done to her she casts herself in a good light and those around her (especially Mrs van Daan) in a bad light.
● Ask the children to discuss interesting language features in this extract. They should note the exclamation marks, strong words and adjectives used. Make any other annotations about expressive language.

● Challenge them to note any clichés or worn phrases ('grin and bear it', 'taking... lying down', 'wasn't born yesterday' and several others).
● Record these language features on photocopiable page 17.
● Ask them to note the force of the passage and how it builds up to the final sentences using the words 'seethe' and 'scold', before the strength of 'explode with pent-up rage'. *Is Anne using such words because she genuinely feels like that, or is she using them for dramatic effect?*

> **Differentiation**
> **For older/more confident learners:** Note the list of adjectives ('bad-mannered', 'headstrong', and so on) and write definitions for them. Are they repetitive or distinctive?
> **For younger/less confident learners:** List the exclamation marks, question mark and ellipsis used in the extract. Discuss with a partner why Anne uses this punctuation and whether it is effective.

Plot, character and setting

Written to last

> **Objective:** Explore the notion of literary heritages and understand why some texts have been particularly influential or significant.
> **What you need:** Copies of the Diary, flipchart.
> **Cross-curricular links:** ICT.

What to do
● Ask the children to consider what it is about Anne's Diary which makes it particularly influential and significant.
● Challenge them to think of ideas about the plot, character and setting which have made it an essential book for children and adults since 1947. Record these on the flipchart.
● Now ask the children to look at the Diary and make notes about those entries which make the book stand out as a particularly significant text. They may consider the quality of the writing, the historical context of Anne's entries, the details about Anne's relationship with Peter or anything else which they think makes the book stand out.

● Ask them why this book stands out from other diaries, other accounts of life during wartime and other memoirs of young people. Discuss how there are many aspects of the Diary which, taken as a whole, make it one of the most important books of the twentieth century.
● Discuss the fact that the book has been read and studied all over the world and has had an impact and influence on people of all ages from many different backgrounds.

> **Differentiation**
> **For older/more confident learners:** Use the internet to research other diaries and recounts written by children during war, and say why these are important, but are unlikely to have the 'success' of Anne's Diary.
> **For younger/less confident learners:** Use the internet to research the sales and translation figures for the *Diary of a Young Girl*, and report the findings to the rest of the class.

Character traits

> **Objective:** Retrieve, select and describe information.
> **What you need:** Photocopiable page 18, copies of the Diary.

What to do
● Ask the children to think carefully about character traits for the people in the Annexe.
● Use a talk partner to discuss them. Point out that they should consider any similarities and differences. Does the captivity bring out some of the same traits in any of the characters?
● Ask the children to explain what a Venn diagram is, and whether we could use one to examine character traits.
● Show a large version of Photocopiable page 18 and tell the children the top diagram is where they will write notes about Anne and Peter, and the bottom one is where they will write notes about

Anne's mother and Mrs van Daan. They should use copies of the text to find the information, then write it in note form.
● Remind them that the central section of the diagram is for shared characteristics.
● When the children have completed the task, ask about any difficulties they faced. Was there an issue about characters changing over a period of time? Open the discussion to talk about how the captives' personalities change during the time in the Annexe.

> **Differentiation**
> **For older/more confident learners:** Challenge the children to make a Venn diagram with three intersecting circles to study other characters.
> **For younger/less confident learners:** Children can make their own Venn diagrams about the characters which they know best, but they should still be guided towards the text for information retrieval.

Plotting

Use the table below to record the dates of Diary entries and the events which Anne describes happening outside and inside the Annexe. Pay close attention to the progress of the war.

Date of diary entry	Events outside the Annexe	Events inside the Annexe

Family matters

	Father (Otto)	Mother (Edith)	Sister (Margot)
Appearance (what they look like, what they wear, how they move)			
Actions (what they do)			
Talk (what they talk about)			
Summary			

PHOTOCOPIABLE

■SCHOLASTIC
www.scholastic.co.uk

READ & RESPOND: Activities based on The Diary of a Young Girl

SECTION
4

Word Wall

Write down any interesting language features from the extract in this 'wall'.
Note the string words, adjectives, cliches and so on.

Character traits

● Complete this Venn Diagram for the personality traits of Peter and Anne. Write about Anne in the left circle, and Peter in the right. Shared traits should go in the middle.

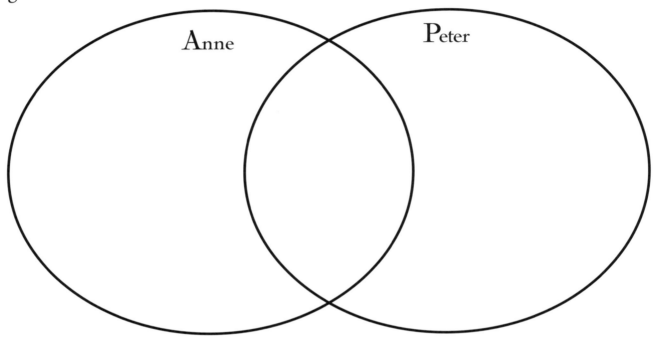

Anne   Peter

● Now complete this one for Anne's mother and Mrs van Daan.

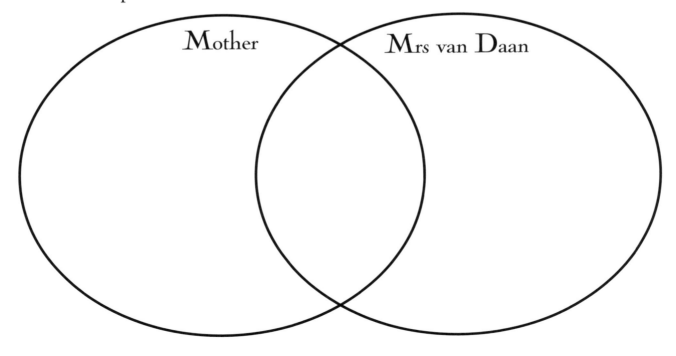

Mother   Mrs van Daan

SCHOLASTIC
www.scholastic.co.uk

Talk about it

Questions and answers

> **Objective:** Use and explore different question types.
> **What you need:** Photocopiable page 22.
> **Cross-curricular link:** Drama.

What to do
● Tell the children to think about the different people who lived in the Annexe. How much do we know about them and are there some things we would like to find out?
● Ask the children to consider open and closed questions. Explain the terms. Suggest that they may find out more by asking open questions.
● Challenge the children to think of themselves as journalists interviewing one of the people in the Annexe. What would they want to find out? What sort of questions might lead to good answers?
● Now suggest that they are going to interview one of the people at different stages of their stay in the Annexe: on entering, at Christmas 1943 and when they are betrayed.
● Ask the children to use Photocopiable page 22 to write down some questions.
● Explain how they should have some questions as prompts but must then be free to follow up what the interviewee has said or revealed.
● Suggest some go in to role as Ann or Peter and the other children interview them.
● Show some examples to the rest of the class.

> **Differentiation**
> **For older/more confident learners:** Question more than one person at the same time. Note the interaction between the people being interviewed.
> **For younger/less confident learners:** Work in pairs to interview people. Rehearse questions before the interview, and find out some general biographical information by asking closed questions (such as, place of birth, age, nationality).

The rights of the child

> **Objective:** Reflect on how working in role helps to explore complex issues.
> **What you need:** Copies of the UN Convention on the Rights of the Child (you can find a summary of it at http://www.everychildmatters.gov.uk/strategy/uncrc/atricles/), flipchart.
> **Cross-curricular links:** PSHCE, Drama.

What to do
● Ask the children to consider what rights and responsibilities they have. Record these on the flipchart. Now ask them to consider the rights and responsibilities of children in the 1940s in general, and the case of Anne Frank in particular.
● Are they aware of any laws which promote these rights? Mention the Human Rights Act. This was signed by 21 countries in 1951 as a direct result of the human rights abuses during WW II.
● Now mention the UN Convention on the Rights of the Child and give the children copies.
● Consider which articles are relevant to Anne.
● Organise the children in mixed ability groups to explore these issues using drama. Explain that two people from each group are to take the role of lawyers explaining to a court which of Anne's rights have been violated. The other members of the group are to direct and support the role-players.
● Present the lawyer's findings to the class. Which lawyers put the best case and why?
● Now ask the children to explain how the role play helped them to explore the issues.

> **Differentiation**
> **For older/more confident learners:** Discuss and present new articles for the Convention, using formal language in the third person.
> **For younger/less confident learners:** Describe, in their own words, which articles are most important to them, and which might have helped Anne Frank.

Talk about it

To publish or not to publish

> **Objective:** Use a range of oral techniques to present persuasive arguments and engaging narratives.
> **What you need:** Photocopiable page 23.
> **Cross-curricular link:** Drama.

What to do
● Organise a whole-class discussion about the original publication of the Diary.
● Explain how Miep Gies found the scattered pages of the Diary and saved them in a desk drawer. After the war she gave them to Otto, Anne's father, who edited the entries before trying to get the Diary published.
● Ask the children to consider why it was difficult to get the Diary published.
● Challenge the children to think of the publication issue from two viewpoints: that of Otto and that of potential publishers.
● Show the children Photocopiable page 23 and tell them they are to make notes from two viewpoints: that of Otto and that of a publisher. Ask them to consider why anyone would want to read such an account shortly after the war. Ask them to suggest what Otto might say to convince a publisher – and why a publisher might steer clear of such a book.
● Tell the children they must think about why the book was important then, and why it is important now.
● After completing the prompt sheet, arrange the children, in pairs, to act out a meeting between Otto and a publisher. Suggest they use the prompts as needed.

> **Differentiation**
> **For older/more confident learners:** Ask the children to switch roles mid-way through the exercise and to develop the other person's argument.
> **For younger/less confident learners** Arrange children in groups (as an editorial board) to reduce pressure on individuals asking/answering questions.

Reasons

> **Objective:** Present a spoken argument, sequencing points logically, defending views with evidence and making use of persuasive language.
> **What you need:** flipchart, pens and paper.
> **Cross-curricular link:** PSHCE.

What to do
● Tell the children they are going to use persuasion to counter an invented argument. Then say it has been decided that schoolchildren will no longer study Anne Frank's *The Diary of a Young Girl*. Ask the children to generate reasons why it should still be studied and record these on the flipchart.
● Now ask the children to write any other reasons down on their own sheets of paper, asking them to write clear and concise reasons why it should still be studied. Tell the children to consider what the Diary offers us, not only from a socio-political viewpoint, but also as an example of a young person's writing.
● Challenge the children to orally rehearse their arguments with a partner for five minutes.
● Invite volunteers to offer their arguments to the rest of the class, allowing another five minutes' preparation in small groups, with the other members of the group supporting the volunteers, offering their own suggestions.
● Ask the children to present their persuasive arguments to the rest of the class, and offer constructive feedback at the end of the session.

> **Differentiation**
> **For older/more confident learners:** During the presentations, ask these children to record the most succinct and powerful argument points.
> **For younger/less confident learners:** Pair children with more fluent speakers on the understanding that both should help to develop the arguments.

Talk about it

The inner voice

> **Objective:** Use the techniques of dialogic talk to explore ideas, topics or issues.
> **What you need:** Photocopiable page 24, enlarged copy of the Diary extract.

What to do

● Read an enlarged copy of the Diary extract, February 23 1944.

● Talk about the notion of internal voice, and explain to the children that a writer or character may be writing or saying one thing but meaning something different. Ask the children if they can think of any examples of this.

● Discuss whether Anne censored herself in her Diary. (Comments about her mother, for example, suggest she did not.)

● Ask the children to consider and make notes on Photocopiable page 24 about what Anne and Peter are thinking and feeling at that time.

● Now suggest ways in which the children can use Drama to explore this further. Have one person reading extracts from the Diary while another voices the things Anne is not committing to paper. Is it possible to find such extracts?

● In small groups, assign some children to enact the scene while others do alternative voice-overs, allowing time for rehearsal.

● Allow the children to explore dramatic techniques and present the results to the rest of the group. Present in an interesting dramatic way and share with the rest of the group.

> **Differentiation**
> **For older/more confident learners:** Take the role of directors and suggest different ways of presenting the thoughts and feelings of both Anne and Peter.
> **For younger/less confident learners:** Practise the piece in order to present it to other children in Assembly.

Family discusssion

> **Objective:** Adopt a range of roles in discussion, including acting as spokesperson, and contribute in different ways such as promoting, opposing, exploring and questioning.
> **What you need:** large sheets of paper, marker pens.

What to do

● Tell the children they are going to discuss the feelings of the Frank family. How do Margot, Otto and Edith feel during the years Anne kept her Diary? Explain that Anne attributes things to them but we are only given one side of the story.

● Split the class into groups of four or five, and give each group large sheets of paper and marker pens. Assign the role of scribe to a quick and willing writer.

● Explain that the groups are going to discuss and make notes about the family members. Circulate among the groups, listening to the discussions. The children are to write down as many character traits, based on their recall of the text, as possible.

● Talk about the importance of building on other children's ideas, and ask the children to develop their discussions of the characters to benefit the whole group.

● Conclude by sitting the class in a circle. Ask each child to offer a comment on each character. See how far round the circle you can go with each child thinking of different character attributes. Which characters have fewer comments and why?

> **Differentiation**
> **For older/more confident learners:** Act as spokesperson for their groups and present the findings to the rest of the class at the end of the session, summing up how the arguments developed.
> **For younger/less confident learners:** Children take on roles as questioners, asking 'Why?' for every point raised to ensure the discussion points are strong.

Talk about it

Questions and answers

Choose a person from the Annexe you wish to interview. In each box write down some key questions.

Interviewer:	Interviewee:

Key questions for Interview 1 (on entering the Annexe)

Key questions for Interview 2 (Christmas 1943)

Key questions for Interview 3 (the Annexe is discovered)

To publish or not to publish

Use the columns below to write notes giving arguments for the publication –
or not – of Anne's Diary in the period shortly after the war. Try to offer
balanced and convincing arguments for both sides. Use the notes as prompts
when acting out a meeeting between Otto and a publisher.

Otto's point of view	The publisher's point of view

Talk about it

The inner voice

Read diary extract Wednesday, 23 February 1944. Think carefully about the feelings Peter and Anne have for each other, and complete the table below.

Anne's thoughts, feelings, words	Peter's thoughts, feelings, words

SCHOLASTIC
www.scholastic.co.uk

READ & RESPOND: Activities based on The Diary of a Young Girl

Get writing

Mother and daughter

> **Objective:** To explore point of view, to write in role.
> **What you need:** Enlarged copy of Photocopiable page 28, copies for children, copies of Diary entry.

What to do
● Read the extract from Anne's Diary entry of Saturday, 3 October 1942.
● Ask the children to consider the subjective nature of the Diary and the fact it is all from Anne's viewpoint. There is no opportunity for anyone mentioned to respond.
● Now ask the children what they think about Anne's comments about her mother in this section.
● Remind the children how Otto, Anne's father, edited the Diary before taking it to a publisher. The 1947 version did not contain many sections where Anne was critical of her mother.
● Hand out Photocopiable page 28 and tell the children they are going to write as Anne's mother. Discuss how they might do this. Talk about using evidence from the text, along with their imaginations.
● Ask the children if they think Edith is aware of Anne's feelings and thoughts about her. Does this awareness, or lack of it, tell us something about her character that might help us to write from her point of view?
● Tell the children to complete both boxes on the Photocopiable sheet.
● As a plenary, ask the children to read their writing, and discuss the different interpretations of this character.

> **Differentiation**
> **For older/more confident learner:** Writing as Edith, compose pen portraits of the other members of the Annexe.
> **For younger/less confident learner:** After hearing the extract read at the beginning of the session, write an entry in their own words.

Step up to the challenge

> **Objective:** Set their own challenges to extend achievement and experience in writing.
> **What you need:** Copy of the Diary, simple apertures (pieces of cardboard with small slits/openings), paper and pens.

What to do
● Read the Diary entries from 23 February and 18 April 1944, focusing on those parts which mention the horse chestnut tree.
● Explain that this was one of the few examples of nature and the outside world which Anne Frank could see. Discuss how the tree became an important symbol for both Anne and people who later read her Diary. Anne wrote of the hope the tree gave her.
● Explain what an aperture is and ask the children to use one to look at different points in the classroom, and out of the window.
● Ask the children to work with a partner to talk about what they have seen and to report back.
● Now tell the children they are going to look through the aperture and write about what they see. They are free to choose any form or style of writing, but they must attempt to challenge themselves.
● Tell them to have the courage to fail. You are not expecting a finished, polished piece of writing, but rather a brave step into the unknown.
● Ask willing volunteers to read their writing to the rest of the class.

> **Differentiation**
> **For older/more confident learner:** Ask the children to consider which elements of their writing need strengthening and to focus on these when they write.
> **For younger/less confident learner:** Suggest a form or genre to the children before they write and offer sample openings.

Get writing

First, second, third

> **Objective:** Sustain form in narrative, including use of person.
> **What you need:** Copies of the Diary.

What to do
● Ask the children what they understand by the terms 'first person' and 'third person', and to clarify the meanings.
● Now discuss the difference between 'biographical' and 'autobiographical' writing.
● Explain that they will read entries from Anne's Diary and choose one to change from a piece of first person autobiographical writing to third person biographical writing.
● Now tell the children they will be working in pairs, where one acts as the scribe and the other checks the conventions are being adhered to.
● Hand out copies of the Diary to each pair and give them five or ten minutes to choose a suitable entry.
● Now ask them to change it to the third person.
● Suggest that they read it aloud to make sure it comes across as a fluent third person piece.
● Ask selected children to read both the original version and their new third person version. Discuss the effects of the changes and whether the children think the writing has been improved in any way. Ask the children if they think the 'distance' third person writing gives can be useful in this context.

> **Differentiation**
> **For older/more confident learner:** Write the extract in the second person, using 'you' and discuss with the rest of the class how this affected the writing.
> **For younger/less confident learner:** Direct these children to simple, short entries from Anne's Diary which you know could easily be changed into the third person.

The Annexe

> **Objective:** Experiment with different narrative forms and styles to write stories.
> **What you need:** Photocopiable page 29, on A3 if possible; copies of the Diary.

What to do
● Ask the children to look at the diagram of the Annexe in diary entry Thursday 9th July, 1942. Talk through the different rooms and ask the children to recall events that happen in the different places.
● Now ask the children to think about feelings associated with each part of the Annexe. Offer sample questions such as 'How does Anne feel in her bathroom?'
● Give the children copies of the photocopiable page and tell them to find references to different rooms and areas in the text and write in feelings and references in the plan of the house.
● Now tell the children they are to write a story based on one of the rooms and the feelings connected to it.
● Challenge the children to write in a different form or style. Suggest they write from the point of view of the tin tub which is used as a bath, or as the cooker which notices the different ways different characters use it and behave. Alternatively, they could personify an emotion, such as hope or sadness, as it moves its way through the house.

> **Differentiation**
> **For older/more confident learner:** Challenge the children to find out and write down which rooms have the most positive and negative associations for Anne.
> **For younger/less confident learner:** Remove the necessity to write text references on the plan. Use the children's own recollections of events and feelings in the Annexe as the starting point.

Get writing

Know your market

> **Objective:** Write about a text, taking account of the needs of others who might read it.
> **What you need:** Folded sheets of A4 and A3.

What to do

● Ask the children if they know that books are sometimes published in two editions: one for adults and one for younger people. Do they know of any examples?

● Now discuss what appears on the cover of a book: illustrations, the blurb giving information about the book and the 'puff', which may include quotations trying to sell the book.

● Ask the children to imagine if a publisher were to do this for Anne's Diary. Do they think this is a good idea? Anne's Diary has universal appeal, so why would a publisher do this? (Explain that publishers need to reach as wide an audience as possible to sell more books.)

● What sort of blurb and puff would you include for the different editions?

● Ask the children to work in pairs. Give each child a folded sheet of A4 to act as a book cover. One of them will plan a cover for younger people and the other will make a mock-up of a cover for adults. Ask the children to discuss their ideas before writing.

● Finally, ask if the Diary is for girls, boys or both. Would it be marketed differently if it was aimed at one gender?

> **Differentiation**
> **For older/more confident learner:** In mixed gender pairs, have the boy design a cover aimed at girls and the girl design a cover aimed at boys. Allow time to discuss and challenge any stereotypes raised.
> **For younger/less confident learner:** Assign individual children to concentrate on a particular aspect of the cover: the design, blurb or puff. Record on large sheets of paper for display and use in the plenary.

'All different and yet the same'

> **Objective:** To establish, balance and maintain viewpoints.
> **What you need:** Photocopiable page 30, flipchart.

What to do

● Read the quotation from Photocopiable page 30: 'We all live with the objective of being happy, our lives are all different and yet the same.'

● Ask the children to explain what they understand by this quotation.

Discuss how there were many aspects to Anne's character and explain that she had many of the same concerns as young people in the 21st century.

● Ask them to brainstorm any ideas about the similarities and differences between Anne's life and the lives of people they know. Record these examples on the flipchart.

● Challenge the children to think of current examples of children who are in danger.

Sensitively refer to recent and ongoing wars and conflicts which affect children.

● Ask the children to consider all the simple everyday domestic challenges which they share with Anne – privacy in the bathroom, a space to do their homework and leave their things.

● Show them Photocopiable page 30 and tell them they are to use the table to make notes about the similarities and differences between the lives of a child today and Anne Frank's life.

● Suggest they use these notes to write a balanced piece about the differences and similarities.

> **Differentiation**
> **For older/more confident learner:** Ask the children to personalise the writing, so they are comparing their own life with Anne's.
> **For younger/less confident learner:** Completion of the grid is the activity here: there is no need to write further, unless the children complete the grid well and want to attempt further writing.

Mother and daughter

Imagine you are Anne's mother, Edith, and complete the following sections using your knowledge of text and your imagination. Think carefully about Edith's 'voice'.

What Anne thinks about me:

What I think about Anne:

The Annexe

You are going to use this plan as a starting point for writing about the feelings Anne associates with different parts of the Annexe. Make notes on the plan to help your writing.

Third floor

Second floor

First floor

Remember – On the above plan write down any feelings or thoughts associated with any of the rooms in the Annexe. You may concentrate on one floor only if you wish.

'All different and yet the same'

'We all live with the objective of being happy,
our lives are all different and yet the same.'
Anne Frank

● Use the table below to make notes about the similarities and differences between the lives of a child today and Anne Frank's life.

Same/similarities	Different

● Now develop these ideas into a balanced and carefully-structured piece of writing which clearly shows that you have understood both the similarities and differences between your life and Anne's life.

Assessment

Assessment advice

The Diary of a Young Girl deals with difficult themes. As well as the 'outside' context of Nazism, hatred and intolerance, there are also the internal struggles Anne has as a young woman in a particular place at a particular time.

These two assessment activities deal with both sides of the Diary.

As with all aspects of the work undertaken when studying Anne Frank's writing, sensitivity is essential for the teacher and other adults in the classroom. Activities should only be undertaken with careful thought and planning.

The first activity asks children to write about the different characters in the Annexe in the style of Anne's Diary, and is designed to show their understanding of both content and form.

The second activity asks children to demonstrate knowledge of the context of the Diary and Anne's emotions during her time in the Annexe.

Anne's Diary

Assessment focus: To write in the style of a known author.
What you need: A variety of easily-found objects and pictures; news and characters' names on slips of paper.

What to do

● Tell the children they are going to write a diary entry in the style of Anne Frank's.
● Give the children objects to include in the entry – these could be fruits, a pack of colouring pencils, sweets, a birthday card, a cat basket.
● Provide news about Nazi success or defeat.

● Now give them three slips of paper with names of three people from the Annexe.
● Ask them to begin and end their diary entry as Anne does, and to write in the same style. Use the mix of the specific and the general, have the characters asking themselves or Kitty questions and talk about the other characters in the house.

Differentiation
For older/more confident learners: The children could write the entry for the next day, showing any consequences from the previous entry.
For younger/less confident learners: Write a shorter entry and give the opening/closing lines as scaffold.

Inside outside

Assessment focus: To recall some of the main events of the Diary and to explain how Anne coped with them.
What you need: Photocopiable page 32.

What to do

● Explain to the children that they are going to consider the pressures and events that were happening inside and outside the Annexe during Anne's time hidden away. (For example, inside: disagreements with the rest of the residents, mixed emotions towards her family, and her emotions towards Peter as she is growing up.)

● Ask them to also consider how Anne copes with the pressures (one main way is by writing in her Diary.)
● Write the children's suggestions down on a whiteboard or flipchart.
● Ask the children to complete Photocopiable page 32, using words, pictures or symbols.

Differentiation
For older/more confident learners: The children could write complete sentences, using connectives such as 'however', 'although', and so on.
For younger/less confident learners: Provide the notes on a whiteboard or flipchart for reference.

Inside outside

At the top of the page make notes about events that are happening inside and outside the Annexe which are having an effect on Anne. At the bottom of the page write notes about how she finds a release for her anxieties and frustrations. You may use small symbols or pictures to illustrate your points.

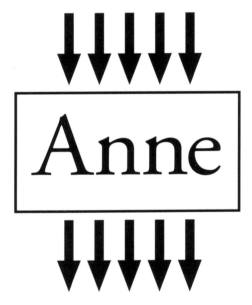